# FIRM OF STEP

# Firm of Step

LORRAINE ANSELL

ISBN 978-1-8383830-0-8

Lorraine Ansell
lorraineansellauthor@gmail.com
www.lorraineansellauthor.com

*Step wide, step close, step together for the comforts will envelop you always.*

# *PROLOGUE*

"Firm of Step" is a collection of words that have come together after four seasons of experience. Each short poem features unpolished stones that can only shine once you have read them.

Formed from daily life, Lorraine Ansell, has shaped characters into form and re-arranged them into stories. Short and perfectly formed into the paragraphs and pages you see here.

"Firm of Step" first started decades ago and it was only when a walk through a busy town centre graveyard, that illuminated a literary path that Lorraine would tread like a cat alighting upon a piano key.

These twenty two especially selected poems and musings have been curated from many words and are now showcased for your enjoyment.

Take what you need from each poem or story and thank you for taking the time to discover new arrangements.

# FIRM OF STEP

Firm of Step and light of mind
I come to you
with thoughts that shine.

The heady passage of my heart
Finally allows reining control
To the fleeting feet from within.

When the tide breaks
The pebbles and stones
Crumble to specks
To surface again, to sense the spark
Burst and pour forth a fiery essence.

Upon the screen, background anew
Fawn no longer
Memory revoked, a rush to the heart
Solitude rains.

# UPTICK

Blue it glows, blue it beckons
A tease, making me feel small, swamped,
The meaning lost to the swipe
Each flick a false validation.

Beware the blue, the call of fiction
The social siren drawing you into
A room full of promised praises
The fortune, a friction.

Slivers glitter with treasures from beyond
All life first in show
Soon, the parade turns into another
The tribes are clear.

The blue blooms and tie after tock after tick
The splice aches, retreat, regroup
Release and feel the ground.

# *DRESSED*

The brown dress, colour flecked shone to me in the
basement cave

The shape of covered flesh tugged at my own

The hope that had betrayed me crept back to tease me

What had I found?




A look, a smile, an understanding connection,

A freedom to cross every sand drawn line,

Losing myself into a paradise,

What had I bound?

The hunt awakens and I spark the fire for simple sur-
vival,

The blue green hues seek out the answers I have,

Diving right in, feeling the softest of pink suede,

What was that sound?




Exquisite art full of tender pain,

Skin and soul on display, the arena life on the screen

Pixels spinning together in the cornucopia of touch,

I have lost but I am ground.

# *RED PAPER CRINKLES*

The red paper crinkles, below a thousand strands,
The quietness of the daylight, betrays the silence.


All screens gleam, screams from within,
Contained by yet another sourdough batch.


The circus distends,
The circuit frays until only sparks poke through,
A rare agreement unites us all,


This year is different, difficult, divine
With the switching of seasons,


We can no longer count on the benign
The truth becomes a reflection of self


Green replaces grey, replaces green
Endless scrolls of characters.

Each of us grasping onto each and with every ping
A warmth creeping in with each.


What brews this day?
Perhaps time for space for play?
A walk away, no wheels to carry us away.
Stay still, stay home, stay well.

# *MOLASSES*

I summon from all corners, the light, the dark, the pleasure, the pain.

Fundamentals strain together, mixed together ready for piping afresh,
I read from the book, the black ants darting back and forth for a sensual rumba,

Pouring from the leaves, a larder full of emotions become solid form.

Tendrils billow around me, reaching further than before, entwining around desires
I cast with delicate ease, millennia in the making with a fanned approach.

The turning colour wheel spins with honey
I watch, for now the joy burns matching the light in your eyes.

# BE MY SPACE

Here, I belong, being totally, solely, truthfully
The grey gives way to a rainbow gouache
of movement,

I fly to space and back,
the ticket is infinite and the joy
cracking into shape.

A multitude to voices summon me to stand
and I more than look,
I feel, I am,

I burst from the pleasure of recognition,
from the beauty that I have found my feet,
from down to up.

Be it partitioned, the floor still holds me
but I am free to be carried around it,

In my space, I am infinite, a truth that
only me myself and I know.
The flow whirls through me
and hours have passed by
Me.

# *MANTRA*

Over, over, over again I hear
Open, closed, open, closed I sense.

The confusion envelopes me and I collapse
From the effort to untangle your threads

I thread myself further within
Over, over, over again I feel
The colours unravel, white noise I hear

Dipped into the kaleidoscope I emerge
Stronger with a corps that breaks only
When you want it to

Over, over, over again I see
Deadly signs with a double step
I turn available to march into the unknown

Content only to live this again
When you need me, I am ready.

# *MELODY*

Who are you? And what would you have been?
Something musical for sure.

Something more fitting for this hyper realist world.
What tunes would you have played?

Playing them daily on every instrument,
you would have grasped inside and pulled out
beams of sound,
waves splitting atoms until they alignment.

Who would have been your friends? Where would
you have lived?
I look at the sky we shared and see a cloud.

Is that you?
I tumble over the pathways losing myself until I
find you.
A river of sound that you called to me in a
myriad of ways that I have only just heard.

Finally you and I are to indulge together.
United and apart.

# *PESTO & PEARLS*

As another normal day curls away to sleep,
I remain wrapped up in a pillow of adoration.
The door calls to me and a pot of green gold awaits,
for me to stir it into action.

Warmth floods my body and a love that allows me
to breathe with ease, plunges me deep into a river
of gratitude.
Here before me simplicity of life itself,
green and rich.

As another normal night wipes away into
movement,
I welcome the solitude of life & each grit moment.
A single stone, milky white, held aloft by
golden chains claims me
and again I feel that translucent love,
waving over me like a sheet of completion.

The continual striking blends together until there
is nothing, but pesto and pearls.

# *ENTRANCE*

I feel like it bursts out of me continually.

A rich never ending exhausting supply of power that rides on wave after wave.

Infinite and mine and yet I feel frightened.

As when you watch the sea a sense of utter surrender.


I walk the fine line of fear and I dance into the power.

I am afraid to embody it, I am fearful that I am not yet quite worthy or ready.

I feel my audience watching me awaiting my arrival.

I bow my head.


My patient ancestors nod slowly and now I feel joy tinged with sadness.

I grieve for the friend I knew, I pity the lover I was.

It is time. I enrobe myself with the cloak of many colours, the embroidery a neutron network of power and ability and I settle into it.


Finally wearing the finest of wares.

Myself. I am here.

# *BEWITCHED*

Casting, I seek both narrow and wide
A web with tendrils awaiting every move
Feline patience, every muscle primed
Time passes, counting up and down.

One eye on the beat, another on the sweep
How long has it been?
The centuries pass in moments, a blink
There with a key step change.

I catch on, a new rhythm and I relax
I pull on the strings,
My doll like visage smiles,
Eyes wide and I feel familiarity

Heart open, I await, warm and agile
Time has stopped and started along with the corps
The harvest begins and I stretch to receive it.

# *LOCKDOWN LIGHTS*

The golden fruit, dappling in the shady sun
The black fur coat, draped unwillingly
The warm current, blowing messily
Two choices, accept or not and yet the green slashes spring into life calling me, grabbing me more, moving me truthfully.

Tinny taps and cat paws have rendered my identity,
The rope feeling welcome and homely within my hands, the rainbow fabric yielding into shape from my fingers, the silver dart galloping piecing the feelings into smoke.

Moments stretch as I orientate and power fills my veins, peace reaches me,
the silence shattering
I feel my ears twitch, my heart race, my brain frost and fizzle
For in this roar, I have been found.

# *UPROAR*

Rich, dark, viscous,
A fluidity that I want to be stopped by,
Then turned and restarted
The ruby red shine blares at me,
Rendering me blank
A neutral state that I want to drown in,
I swallow it whole, the fluid colour, enrobing me,
And a queen I am.
Now cleansed, spectre began whole.

# *THE EMPTY STAGE*

The stage is empty, company full but vacant
Vacant due to your absence
A thousand stars switch off.
A single tear for when you appear
It snows a palace within me
I shake at the cold, wonder in the coolness
For when you shine, I shatter,
The blood red line you deign to showcase
Draws me to safety
When the chorus swells
I join in, ready for the music
In the wings, I prepare
Your hair a beacon framing
A tanned crisp face, falling, casting shadows
In the wings, I watch
Long clean lines, kick up from below
And the darkness vanishes from your limbs
All directions again.
As the world spins, I find your eyes
Dark pools of liquid navy
Oil together with gold until it burns

# *SPIRAL*

Chains that are freeing
Punches that are kisses
I float into form, a flicker back into force
My hand, an aching extension
Beauty and joy in naked core
I reach to grasp and continually feel
Lights gather sending me colours
One and one and two to centre me
Now the spiral begins and up to the box I look
Aiming for the doors
Twisting like silk to the posters
Bonded together by waves

# SOUND OF SILENCE

The dial shakes and yet I do not say it
The line quivers and still I don't admit it
The beading multiplies and finally I allow it
A chasing step on grey cylinder
Capturing cantering colours within a hanger of light
A beam trained on practice
As I long for perfection
The focus is what I allow
To be seen, to be watched
Messy shapes, staccato frames, clumsy catches
Cacophony pouring embraces the air
Shapes surround us in swirls
Exhausted but happy, the silence is filled with sound.

# THE WATCHER

Through the pixels I watch
You
Through the portal I feel
You
Through the plate I am
You
Completely

# SHELTER

The triangle appears and with it the circle
I burrow secure within
A knowledge burns me to ash
The warmth settles deeply
Until it radiates like a stray dogs dreams
A joy longer than before
This rectangle housing me and I stretch up,
Reaching an apex,
A star bursts ahead and the confetti lights the
path.

# THE LIGHT ORDER

My fingers stretch out before me
I feel that strength as each unfurls
The light you gave me, pin pricks in the dark
Newly surround me, glowing with rising strength
I watch and I am watched
For now I am the keeper
Of the lights, of dreams and our only love
The current takes me, the colours a collision
Footfalls gently pad and awake our minds
The white mask disappears and the rainbow shim-
mers through
The beauty of the beat harnesses the other
For now I am the keeper
OF the lights, of the shapes, of the sounds
The ripples are felt, right at the heart
Never quite reaching an end
A change of direction, a direct move
Always together, constantly unique
For now I am the keeper,
Of the lights, of the lights, forever

# *MAKE ME*

When I awoke you shaped me
When I fell, you made me carry,
When I tried, you made me succeed
You turned the light on with each step,
The shape of you I turned into,
The discovery of me, I bounced
Despite the crowning, we continue
The feelings gather and grow
The bloom from white to red brings clarity
Finally on my feet,
The tender look of a mother to a child,
I became the dance for me.

# *LIGHT SHOW*

As we whirl in group formation,
Tightly knit we fly,
We bend and roll, like water around rocks,
I feel each beat, each life and every story
Like geese we flock, feathers filled with the fresh-
est air
We parade and we sparkle, brush, walk, look, smile
and sing
The heat makes us giddy and we carry on
The ensemble is complete
The lights track us and through them we twirl
Holding each position, we force our way through
Dressed to fit, made up to face the night,
And as the tunes stop, we hold, completed.

# PART TIME LOVER

Down the silver snake goes.
The grates increasingly rubbing at my patience.
Down by degrees, down into the voids.
The end is almost insight.
I hold onto the well worn rubber
And above the echoed scrapping I hear the beat
Down a scale, up for a chord change
Here two felines tumble with admiration
Clutter into laughter
Brass bold, the throb a reminder
Of joy hidden at the core
Relief of another identity let go.

Each close, each open, each out and in requires a
belief, a risk and a knowing of time and space.
May you find relief in each element.

# *About the Author*

Lorraine Ansell is a global story teller with over twenty years creative narrative experience. She has worked on stories, narratives, tales and copy for decades including for advertisements, brand content and story driven entertainment.

Lorraine has written audio dramas as well as many short stories. She is fuelled by colours and sounds as well as visuals.